Riddles for Kids

100+ trick questions, math games, short brainteasers and fun riddles for smart kids to enjoy with the whole family

By Wonderland For Children

1) Suzy has eight pairs of black gloves and eight pairs of brown gloves in her drawer. In total darkness how many must she take from that drawer in order to be sure of getting a pair that match?

2)Who spends the day at the window, goes to the table for meal and hides at night?

3)When I was 4 years old, My sister was half of my age. Now I am 15 years old. How old is my brother?

4) Two fathers and sons walk into a store. They each buy biscuit worth of $50 but they all spend $150 in total. How is that possible?

5) A butcher has a 37-inch waist around and he is 6 feet tall. What does he weigh?

6) I run it runs, I stop it runs, whatever I do it still keep running

7) Which candle burns longer? A blue candle or a white candle?

8) One Tuesday Clement rode to the bush for three days but he came home on Tuesday. How did he do it?

9) When you take away the whole, but you still have some left over, what do you have?

10) What is mighty than God More bad than devil, If you eat or drink it you die, The poor has it while the rich need have it. What is it?

11) Alex's mother has 4 children:

Emmanuel
Israel
Owen
What is the name of fourth child?

12) Solomon's birthday is the 7th of august yet his better always falls in the winter
Why?

13) A man is 30 years old. A 67 old woman called him "A Father" and a 36-year-old girl called him Father. How is that possible?

14) A prisoner is told, "if you tell a lie we will hang you, if you tell the truth we will shoot you". What can he say to save himself?

15) Wilson subtract 7 from 50. How many times can he subtract 7 from 50?

16) King Batter died 120 years after King Dickson was born. Their combined ages were 100 years. King Dickson died in the year 40 B.C. In what year was king Butter born?

17) There are two birds in front of two other birds. There are two birds behind two other birds. There are two birds beside two other birds. How many birds are there?

18) Nobody can hold me for a minute. What am I?

19) What sprout without a seed and stand without a trunk?

20) I am something, I have a close friend and you can never eat both of us for breakfast; what are we?

21) A donkey is on 20ft chain and what an orange that is 22ft away. How can the donkey get the orange?

22) What can you add to a pail with 500 CL of water to weigh less?

23) Whoever makes it, tells it not, whoever takes it, knows it not, and whoever knows it wants it not. What is it?

24) There is a plane crashed with 50 passengers. The plane crashes on the border of Nigeria and

Ghana. None of the 50 people died. Where will they bury the survivors?

25) A body named Victory was born in 1940. He is celebrating his 18th year's birthday. How is that possible?

26) A man was found dead by hanging himself from the ceiling in an empty room with no doors and window but there is a puddle of water. How did the man die?

27) I know of a word letter three, add two and fewer they will be?

28) What sings and has 10 feet?

29) What is the word inside the riddle?

30) What is the value of ½ of 2/3 of ¾ of 4/5 of 5/6 of 6/7 of 7/8 of 8/9 of 9/10 of 1000?

31) Forward I am heavy, but backward I am not. What am I?

32) I told Rufus "I will bet you $1 that if you give me $2, I will give you $3 in return", Is this a good bet for Rufus to accept?

33) Name consecutive three days without using the word Monday, Tuesday, Wednesday, Thursday, Friday, Saturday and Sunday.

34. Mr and Mrs Ahmed have five sons and each son has one sister. How many people are in Ahmed's family?

35. Two mother and two daughter go shopping. They have $21. How will they share it equally?

36. By 2 am the door bell rings and you wake up Unexpectedly its your family and there are there for breakfast. You have Bread, Honey, Wine, Tea. What will you open first?

37. If it takes three lion to catch three antelopes in three minutes, How many minutes does it takes 99 lion to catch 99 antelopes?

38. A night watch man, while on patrol at night, dreams that the king will die in a plane crash due to the love he has for the king he quickly tell him in the morning, But the king tells him not to worry .He flies away and when he return from the trip, he fires the night watch man. Why does the king fire the night watch man?

39. A forest has no life except for some trees. During a storm, a tree is hit by a lightening and falls. What sound would it make?

40. What does a cockroach and a radio have in common?

41.people buy me to eat, but never eat me, what am I?

42. He married many women but has never been married, what am I?

43. A man was driving a black car with no lights, the moon shown no light, a cat was in the middle of the road, how did he know?

44. What do we cherish most and cannot eat and drink?

45. What is the beginning of life, the end of fall and will and the center of rebellion?

46. What has one eye and cannot see?

47.why didn't the skeleton cross the road?

48.why can't the Christmas tree stand up?

49.what do polar bears take as snacks?

50.what is the favorite music of mummies and ghosts?

51.what type of water can you eat?

52.i am a ball you should never play with?

53.most people sleep when I come?

54.what is known to wash white rocks every morning?

55.what is the collection of math?

56.a book with one page, you read through a whole year, what am I?

57.what stands still and is said to listen?

58.if yesterday was Thursday, what day is tomorrow?

59. What boy wizard magically grew a beard each night?

60. I was born in 1885 and today is my 18th birthday. How come?

61. What comes down and never goes up

62. What does a rain cloud wear under their raincoat?

63. The largest room worldwide is…

64. A house full of meat, no door to go in and eat

65. What is a plumber's favorite song?

66-Some people see me and some don't -What am I?

67- I am a human being I walk with 4 legs what am I?

68- People buy me and stills disturb me for more than 1 hours 30 minutes- What am I?

69- I am an animal, I dies When I give birth to my offspring, what am I?

70- I am something I state the correct time perfectly twice a day- What am I?

71- I am something you write all things with me but longer you write the shorter I goes- What am I?

72- There is an object you use which is 6 letters words but if you remove the first word and replaced it with "c" people hate it- What am I?

73- A man is pushing his car along the road when he comes to a hotel- He shouts, I'm bankrupt- Why?

74- Imagine you bought a bicycle, How will you ride it?

75- I am something I sleeps at night, what am I?

76- The more you use me the more I am reduced. The more I do anything you want- What am I?

77- I am a figure of speech but I don't say the truth- What am I?

78- This place is just like prison, what's the name of the place?

79- Billions of people can't do without me everyday(its not food , water or any basic things-) What I am?

80- How many side does a human being have?

81- I am something people leave me at morning and come back to me at Night- What am I?

82- I work for all living things for 24 hours with no rest- What am I?

83- You have 20 apples in a basket, 20 children come to ask for one each, you will want to give all the apples to each of them, but still keep one inside the basket? How will you do it?

84- Who ate the apple in the garden of Eden?

85- Who eat a lot of iron without getting sick?

86- You can never do without me- What am I?

87- Who can jump higher than hills?

88-I am part of body that remain alive after death?

89- I am something, I like to live in wardrobe What am I?

90- If Loveth's daughter is my daughter's mother, What am I to loveth?

91- What disappears if you say my name?

92- How many seconds are there in a year?

93- There was a plane crash every single person died- Who survive?

94- A man was thirty four on his last birthday and will be thirty six on his next birthday- How is this possible?

95- What can you hold in your right hand, but not in your left?

96- I am 5 letters in word- Remove my first letter, it's a crime, remove the first and last letter, it's a kind of music- What am I?

97- I am an odd number, take away an alphabet and I become even- What am I?

98- If the day after tomorrow is three days before Tuesday, do you know which day is today?

99-A man walked into a party and pours some punch and ice into a cup- He was really thirsty and drank it really fast- Then he left the party- Later he hears everyone at the party died- There was poison in the pouch- How did the man not die if he drank the same punch?

100- What letter of alphabet has lots of water?

101- What do you call 2 witch neighbors?

ANSWERS

1) 9

2) A Fly

3) 13

4) They are three in number (Grandfather,
   Father and Son)

5) He weighs meat

6) My watch

7) None of them

8) Clement rode on Horse named Tuesday

9) Wholesome

10)   Nothing

11)   Alex

12)   Solomon is from Australia

13)   He is a priest

14)   You will hang me

15)   Only once because after that
Wilson will subtract 7 from 63

16)   20 B.C

17)   4 (Position in a square form)

18)   Breath

19)   The world

20)   Lunch and dinner

21)   The chain was not tied to anything

22)   A hole

23)   Fake money

24)   Survivors are alive not dead

25)   He was born on February 29 (leap year) since then there are only 18 leap years

26)   He hung himself using big ice slab which dissolve and form puddle of water

27)   Few

28)   A quintet

29)   The IDDL

30)   100

31)   Ton

32)   No, I win let Rufus win the bet, but he lose $1y

33)   Yesterday, today and tomorrow

34)   9 (parent_ 2, sons_5 while there is only one daughter)

35) $7 each because they are three in number (Grandmother, mother and daughter)

36)   You open your eye first

37)   Three minutes

38)   Because the king realize he was sleeping while on duty that's why he dream about that incidence

39)   None, Sound doesn't exist if it is unheard

40)   Antenna

41)   Dining table

42)   A priest

43)   it was daytime

44)   money

45)   the letter "L"

46)   a needle

47)   because he didn't have any guts

48)   because he has no legs

49)   snowflakes

50)   wrap

51)   watermelon

52)   Eyeball

53)   Night

54)   Toothbrush

55)   A math set

56)   A calendar

57)   Walls

58)   Saturday

59)   Hairy Potter

60)   I was born in room 1885

61)   Rain

62)   Thunderware

63)   Room for improvement

64)   What am i?

65)   Singing in the drain

66)   Ghost

67)   A baby

68)   A football

69)   May flies

70)   Stopped clock

71)   Pencil

72)   Basket (if first word is removed and change to "c" it turns to casket)

73)   He was playing monopoly

74)   Stop imagining

75)   Living thing

76)   Network data

77)   Irony

78)   It's definitely prison

79)   Social media

80)   2 (inside and outside)

81)   Bed

82)   Air

83)   Give 19 apples to 19 children out of 20 of them and give the basket to the last child with the apple in it

84)   He is not me

85)   Rust

86)   Water

87)   Anybody because Hills don't jump

88)   Eyes

89)   Cloth

90)   I am Loveth's daughter

91)   Silence

92)   31536000 seconds

93)   Married couple survives

94)   The man is Thirty Five right now(
His last birthday, He was Thirty four and
next birthday, He will be Thirty six)

95)   Left hand

96)   Grape

97)   Seven

98)   Friday

99)   The poison is in the ice, as he didn't
wait for it to melt

100)   C (sea)

101)   Broom mates

We all hope you have enjoyed those funny
and smart riddles. If you liked them, please
feel free to leave a review.